I Make A Difference!

A Curriculum Guide
Building
SELF-ESTEEM AND SENSITIVITY
in the
Inclusive Classroom

Michele C. Tamaren

Academic Therapy Publications
20 Commercial Boulevard
Novato, California 94949-6191

International Standard Book Number: 0-87879-945-1

1 0 9 8 7 6 5 4 3
0 9 8 7 6 5 4 3 2

CONTENTS

Acknowledgments

It is with sincere appreciation that I wish to thank the Administration and School Committee of the Acton Public Schools for their strong commitment to building self-esteem in our children. Superintendent Robert Kessler, Assistant Superintendent Gary Baker, the Director of Pupil Services, Stephen Donovan, and the Principal of the McCarthy-Towne School, Parker Damon, have enthusiastically supported the objectives set forth in this project. I am grateful, too, for the skilled and sensitive editorial work of Betty Lou Kratoville.

Most especially I wish to thank Fran Leiboff, Chairperson of Elementary Special Education, for her warm encouragement and steadfast guidance in the course of developing programs to enhance the self-esteem of students who learn differently. Her caring assistance since the inception of these projects five years ago has been invaluable.

Walter McGrail, fifth grade teacher at the Gates School, graciously provided me with the opportunity to work with his class in the development of this curriculum guide. The style and direction of the *I Make a Difference!* program were profoundly influenced by the dedication and sensitivity of Mr. McGrail and his students, whose concerns and insights echo throughout this guide.

Paula Centauro	David Cutler
Lisa Davis	Jake Eaker
Benjamin Eckstein	Melissa Fantasia
Courtney Fishbone	Sara Hess
Kara House	Andrew Howison
Jamie Hufnagel	Alyssa Jeanson
Bryan Manter	Jon McGilvra
Kelly Mihalek	Jason Potter
Brian Prentiss	Andrew Rogers
Laura Safran	Joy Sharpe
Susan Shinnick	Charlotte Smith
Carla Torrielli	Mark Zubick

Foreword

In the process of educating today's youth for tomorrow's challenges, educators are becoming more aware of the benefits of heightened personal self-esteem and regard for acceptance of individual uniqueness and differences in others.

A true understanding by students of their own individual strengths, learning style, and self-worth will enable students to seek their greatest potential in both their academic and personal lives.

The *I Make a Difference!* program which was piloted in my classroom during the 1989-1990 school year allowed my students to recognize their own positive attributes and to respect the individual characteristics of others.

During the year, students were able to integrate ideas presented through this curriculum into their daily lives both at school and at home. Parents were highly receptive to the increased awareness of the uniqueness of others exhibited by their children. They were very pleased with the tolerance and acceptance of siblings and peers, as well as strangers, that seemed to become a more natural part of their child's manner.

The students who were involved in this pilot program are now in sixth grade. As I see them interact and dialogue with one another, I sense the continued acceptance of the special qualities that differentiate them. They celebrate each other's successes and feel empathy for one another.

I truly thank them for their wonderful contributions to this guide and believe that their input helped to fashion a program reflective of students' needs and interests. May they carry the tenets of *I Make a Difference!* with them throughout their years.

Also, I want to thank Michele Tamaren for all the time that she spent with my class in the development of this guide. Her manner and style with the children brought out their best.

Lastly, I encourage other educators to utilize the material presented in this guide to promote its principles with their children. The content used to present the major ideals of the *I Make a Difference!* Program may vary with individual teachers and students. I encourage teachers to try the ideas presented in this guide and to integrate their own when the situation warrants it.

Walter McGrail
Gates Elementary School
Acton, Massachusetts

This book is dedicated to the memory of Kara Mroczka (1974-1990), an Acton-Boxborough student whose joyful, caring, and compassionate spirit touched countless lives.

Introduction

As schools prepare students for the dawn of the twenty-first century, leaders in education, business, industry, and government are advocating substantive changes. Cooperative problem solving, creative thinking, and integration of students with all styles of learning into the mainstream classroom are emerging as prime initiatives.

As we move into the next millennium, cooperation, creativity, and inclusion are objectives that have the power to impact not only the schools but society as well. Yet these goals can thrive only in an educational environment that fosters consideration and respect for all persons. Guiding children to honor and to celebrate the integrity of each class member, while recognizing and cherishing their own special value and uniqueness, is the essence of the *I Make a Difference!* program. *I Make a Difference!* emphasizes and teaches that we all count.

Purpose

The *I Make a Difference!* Curriculum Guide, designed for use in grades 4-8, offers a dynamic process approach to enhance cooperation and self-esteem in the inclusive classroom. Educational research reveals that a secure sense of belonging, competence, and self-worth are elements necessary for healthy self-esteem and are prerequisites for the development of academic and social skills (Purkey, 1970). The *I Make a Difference!* program has been formulated to challenge and empower students, regardless of learning style, to grow toward their greatest potential.

Educational initiatives, on both state and federal levels, are urging increased mainstreaming of the child who learns differently. Yet students who experience academic frustration often feel isolated and insecure in the regular classroom. Questions of self-worth and competence, common to all students, are especially prevalent and disturbing to those who are learning disabled. To successfully integrate these youngsters into the mainstream classroom, a milieu must be created in which students acknowledge and support one another's uniqueness and special abilities. Mutual respect then nurtures development of self-regard.

The premise of the *I Make a Difference!* program is that uninhibited learning and solid self-confidence are inspired in the classroom when consideration and respect abound. Students supported by teachers and peers are set free to question, to explore, to grow. Those encouraged to develop and revel in their personal interests and talents will likely acquire essential skills, self-confidence, and a joy in learning. Sensitivity toward others frequently follows.

Objectives

The objectives of this program foster a supportive environment in which teachers, students, and ancillary personnel work cooperatively to assure one another's growth.

1. The ability to make a difference in one's own life and in the lives of others will be recognized.

2. Consideration and respect as behavioral expectations on the part of every class member for all persons regardless of race, religion, age, physical or learning challenges will be established.

3. Sensitivity and awareness of learning style and learning challenges in one's self and others will be developed.

4. The talents and emerging skills in one's self and one's peers will be recognized and celebrated.

Use

The elements of consideration, respect, and personal influence are developed in this program through an interactive process that encourages students to understand and appreciate individual differences. This process stimulates critical thinking and problem-solving skills through the techniques of cooperative learning, brainstorming, experimentation, research, and development of original projects. Teachers and students become facilitators in one another's learning.

Multiple curriculum areas are integrated in this classroom guide which explores interpersonal relations and intrapersonal strengths. As a social science curriculum, it examines psycho-social needs and human emotions. Natural science is incorporated through the study of the learning process, brain function, and perception. The emphasis on language arts and fine arts complement the holistic nature of this guide.

Lessons are presented in the context of eight major themes. The ninth theme is designed to be used as needed to assist individual students to overcome specific classroom difficulties. Sessions of up to one hour may be conducted weekly or more frequently if desired. It is helpful to allot periods during the week for students to work cooperatively in small groups or to give their presentations. While the guide is designed to be used sequentially, it is constructed to encourage flexibility and creative input from both the teacher and students. The program comes to life through the enthusiasm and imagination of the participants.

The true benefit of the *I Make a Difference!* Curriculum Guide is in its impact on the students' attitudes and perceptions of themselves and others. The terms, concepts, and skills developed in the course of this program are most valuable when they become internalized and used as a consistent, natural reference. In guiding students to respect one another and rejoice in themselves, educators offer the basic tools for unlimited, lifelong learning and development.

Those Who Made a Difference

The fabric of this curriculum guide is richly interwoven with threads of caring, love, and concern graciously given by educators, administrators, parents, and students. The School Committee of the Acton Public Schools supported, through Horace Mann and Research and Development Grants, the design of programs to build self-regard in the child who learns differently. The first of three grants allowed for the development and presentation of professional workshops that focused on "Enhancing the Self-Esteem of the Learning Disabled Child in the Classroom." Funding the succeeding year permitted the formulation and implementation of a parent education course entitled "Raising the Child Who Learns Differently." The *I Make a Difference!* Curriculum Guide, which stimulates and fosters sensitivity and self-respect in each of our students, represents the culmination of these works.

During the five years I have had the privilege of pursuing these and related activities, I have witnessed the magic that ensues when children, all children, are honored and encouraged by their teachers and their peers. Designing the *I Make a Difference!* program in concert with Walter McGrail's fifth grade class has been, for me, the highlight of these extraordinary opportunities. The heart of this curriculum guide resonates with the compassion, sensitivity, and celebration of self that the children so freely shared.

Michele Tamaren

Self-Esteem Awareness

CHAPTER 1

Self-Esteem: An Enhancer of Life and Learning

Dejected or delighted, ashamed or assured, self-conscious or self-confident—the quality of one's life is dramatically directed by one's self-esteem. Persons who respect themselves, who are confident of their own abilities, who enjoy a sense of pride are free not only to develop as individuals but to nurture that growth in others as well. One's relationships, goals, accomplishments, and well-being are nourished by an abundant self-regard.

Believing one's self to be worthy and competent are the hallmarks of high self-esteem. Students who possess an appreciation of their own integrity and unique talents exude a creative energy that impels them to set challenging goals and provides the psychic stamina to pursue them. Achieving those aims jointly reinforces the child's skills and sense of self.

However, for our students who do not develop a healthy self-regard, there may be serious ramifications. The child, the family, and society may suffer the consequences (Bryan, 1986). Persons who do not like themselves tend not to have compassion for self or for others. They frequently experience a significant incidence of academic failure, school dropout, mental health problems, drug and alcohol abuse, teen pregnancy, illegal activities, and suicide. In adolescence, intense self-doubt often drives a student to search for a peer group that will validate the young person's very existence. As a result, these individuals tend to be vulnerable to unfavorable influences by those who are themselves alienated and confused.

The disparate quality of life between those possessing high self-esteem and those who harbor a negative self-image may stem, in part, from striking differences in the two belief systems (Weiner, 1974). Individuals who respect themselves tend to feel responsible for their actions and the resultant outcomes. Their determination is fueled by an irrepressible enthusiasm and belief in their self-efficiency. However, persons who feel inferior consign their fate to forces outside themselves. These people dwell in self-imposed prisons, fearful of taking healthy risks and blind to their own potential. Our self-esteem, whether pulsating or paralyzed, largely determines our future.

> Chris, age twenty-one, was seven years old when he, his father, and his six-year-old brother were traveling to school. Their car was struck head on by a drunk driver. Chris's father and brother were killed instantly, and he was rendered coma-

tose. After many weeks in a coma from which the doctors did not expect him to emerge, Chris regained consciousness. The child who was once athletically facile and who learned with ease was now cerebral palsied and learning disabled. One element was left unscarred, however, and that was Chris's enthusiasm for life and his belief in himself. With the support of his devoted mother, caring teachers, and skilled physicians, Chris strove to overcome his disabilities. Today he is a member of the United States Ski Patrol, is an emergency medical technician, lectures to rapt student audiences on the dangers of drug and alcohol abuse, and is studying to become a special educator. Chris's unswerving belief in his own capabilities enriched not only his own life, but is now inspiring others.

Teachers can facilitate their students' discovery of the life-enhancing sense of self-esteem by leading young people to recognize and honor their special worth and competence. Leo Buscaglia, PhD, and former professor of education at the University of Southern California and a nationally prominent writer and lecturer, states, "There is no greater responsibility in the world than being a teacher. Education should be the process of helping everyone to discover his uniqueness, to teach him how to develop that uniqueness, and then to show him how to give it away." In doing so, a teacher may well be touching the child for now and forever, for by enhancing a student's self-esteem, she may be affecting the lives of children yet unborn.

CHAPTER 2

What Is a Learning Disability?

A subtle, cellular difference, played out in the upper reaches of the brain, can contribute to learning differences. One in ten students of average to superior intelligence struggles to learn. A child may be a fluent reader and exhibit impressive mathematical dexterity yet write abysmally. Spelling, handwriting, and organization may suffer. Another student, thirsting to learn, curious about the natural world, may be dyslexic, experiencing severe difficulty in learning to read. Still other children may evidence no apparent academic disorder yet may lack the social skills so vital for acceptance in the classroom. These youngsters, bright, capable, anxious to do well, may be impacted by microscopic or chemical differences in their brains that influence their academic and social styles.

The late neurologist, Norman Geshwind, MD, and his colleague, Albert Galaburda, MD, researchers at Harvard Medical School, have discovered discrepancies in the rate of neurological maturation, brain symmetry, and interconnections in the brains of dyslexics that likely account for learning differences. The left side of the brain, the hemisphere most responsible for language acquisition and production, is often affected. Dr. Geshwind theorized, however, that rather than a disability, these differences may naturally arise from a genetic code guaranteeing diversity of abilities in the population. Often the very people who struggle to learn to read and spell are the individuals who are blessed with unusual talents in other domains. While facility in language is essential for survival in the classroom, other skills have been called upon for survival of the human species.

Adroitness in the visual-spatial and visual-motor domains were essential in the wild and in battle where most of human history has been played. Alvin Toffler, in his book *Future Shock*, explains that in the 800 lifetimes constituting human existence, 650 have been spent in caves. The printed word has been available in just the past six lifetimes and accessible to the masses for only the past four. That which we today consider to be a learning disability may in some individuals be reflective of a highly developed right hemisphere, survival insurance in earlier times. The ability to run quickly, be alert to subtle sounds, and acutely aware of changes in the environment was, for most of the history of mankind, "the right stuff."

There are indeed multiple possible causes of learning disabilities, including prenatal influences, birth trauma, infection, accident, and environmental toxins. Yet forty percent of children with learning differences inherit the genetic instructions from one or both of their parents. Family histories of these individuals also point to a significant incidence of autoimmune disorders such as rheumatoid arthritis and lupus as well as childhood allergies. Dr. Geshwind found in his research that a common etiology of these dysfunctions is the impact of excess testosterone on the language center in the developing fetus. Children and their parents often share similar experiences in the classroom due to their genetically mediated learning styles.

Impact of Learning Disabilities

As learning differences typically, although not exclusively, impact the left hemisphere of the brain, ability to use spoken or written language is often affected. Evidence of this interference may be a compromise in a child's ability to listen, attend, speak, read, write or spell. Frequently these youngsters display problems in the association of letter sounds and symbols. Learning to read phonetically may be extremely challenging for these students. While acquiring a sight vocabulary may be more natural for some, other dyslexic children struggle in this regard as well. Reversal tendencies caused by spatial or sequential dysfunctions can influence the way letters and numbers are perceived. Thus, symbols may appear in backward or transposed position.

In a learning disabled child, mathematical skills also may be impacted. These youngsters may be exceptionally creative in problem solving, yet may experience significant difficulties in memorizing the basic facts. Practical math such as time telling, measurement, and money may be particularly easy or it may be stressful depending on the child's individual learning strengths and weaknesses.

While academic functions may be problematic in the child who learns differently, so may social interactions. Learning disabilities sometimes appear in the guise of social immaturity or ineptness. As language disorders frequently interfere with communication, developing friendships may be one of the more ominous tasks for the learning disabled child. Literal interpretation of idioms or failure to quickly grasp the punchline of a joke may place a chiild in an unenviable position in the hierarchy of the classroom. Confusion as to the implication of body language, facial expression or tone of voice also contributes to the vulnerability of the child who learns differently. These factors, in concert with the tendency in some children to be impulsive and easily distracted, impact on social acceptance and approval.

> Jack, a nine-year-old child who was learning disabled and socially immature, had
> no friends. During one recess he purchased a Frisbee from the school store and
> took it to the side of the courtyard where he played alone. When the whistle blew
> and the children filed back into the school, Jack raised the Frisbee and loudly
> announced, "Look what I stole." His classmates responded in anger, and Jack was

stunned by their reaction. What began as a desperate attempt to secure acknowledgement from his peers again ended painfully for this lonely child.

Creativity in the Learning Disabled Child

While learning disabled children may evidence frustration in the classroom both academically and socially, by the very nature of their neurological make-up they may excel in creative endeavors. Many people who learn differently possess high intelligence and unique problem-solving abilities. These individuals often intuit and reason using a flexible, imaginative style. Both Albert Einstein and Thomas Edison struggled in school due to learning difficulties, yet their differences in learning style likely contributed to their exceptional abilities to integrate information in original and inventive ways. In addition to creative energy, these scientists possessed extraordinary perseverance, which is often a function of the unusual learner. Thomas Edison tested more than five thousand filaments in his quest for electric light before finding the proper element for the incandescent bulb.

Gifts in the arts, sciences, and athletics are often the legacy of people possessing unusual learning styles. Bruce Jenner and Greg Louganis are both Olympic Gold Medalists, and they each experienced severe problems in reading, writing, and spelling. Mr. Louganis, an Olympic diver, didn't learn until his late teens that he was dyslexic. Until then he believed that he was mentally retarded. In fact, his learning style was indicative of a highly developed right hemisphere mediating remarkable spatial perception and extraordinary visual-motor skills. These talents, along with a fierce determination, likely contributed to the gold medal status of both of these athletes. Unusual gifts in the fine arts, such as the keen eye and manual dexterity evidenced by the learning disabled sculptor Rodin, are not infrequently possessed by people with learning differences.

Children who struggle in the classroom often excel musically or theatrically. The right side of the brain, which controls tone, rhythm, and intuitive abilities, appears to be exceptionally strong in many people who have difficulties interpreting written symbols. Cher, Whoopi Goldberg, Sylvester Stallone, and Tom Cruise are successful entertainers who experienced problems in coping with the written word. The commonality of these talented, creative individuals is not so much in their learning disabilities, nor even in their giftedness, but in the pain and confusion suffered by each as a result of feeling incompetent and unworthy in the classroom.

Effects of Learning Disabilities on Self-Esteem

Judge Jeffry Gallet, Family Court Justice of the City of New York, author of five scholarly books, forty articles, and thirty published legal opinions, and professor of law at four major universities, still struggles to read a menu. In a lecture at the Law School of the State University of New York, he spoke of his dyslexia, of graduating last in his college class, and most strikingly of the debilitating lack of self-esteem he suffered due to learning differently. He said,

> I was depressed from kindergarten through law school. In fact I was depressed so long that the presumption was that was the way I was normally. I am not being facetious when I say that. When my depression ended, my mother was amazed to find out who I really was, and so was I. When I use the word depressed, I don't mean a little bit sad. I am talking about clinical symptoms. It's hard to live with everybody telling you that you're stupid all the time.

> My teachers were not surprised to find out that I ended up in court. They were only surprised to find out that I was the judge, not the defendant. I was miserable in school. I hated it, and my teachers knew it. I was a problem child, and I would sit in the back of the room. I talked in class. I did not work up to my potential. My teachers figured I was lazy. You know when you are in school they set up groups, the rabbits, the eagles. I was in the turtles.

> The playground was no easier for me than the classroom. What do you think a social life is like if you think of yourself as the lowest of the low? You are not an athlete; you are not a scholar. You have no self-confidence.

How many students are potential justices or great artists or brilliant scientists or perhaps world leaders who are now shackled by the double binds of learning disablities and low self-esteem? Educators, as significant persons in their students' lives, can help to break those binds and set the children free to find a path which will lead to light and to life.

Refer to Appendix A (page 67) for more information regarding learning disabilities.

CHAPTER 3

The LD Child and Self-Esteem

Learning disabled children frequently harbor a fragile sense of self-esteem. Negative self-judgment, painful peer rejection, and low teacher expectations may sometimes contribute to intense feelings of unworthiness and incompetence. Struggles in the classroom that lead a child to question his inherent abilities and intrinsic value can systematically dismantle a student's confidence as a learner and a human being.

Self-imposed comparisons, both of an academic and social nature, can be particularly disquieting to the child. Observing one's classmates, some not as capable nor creative, assimilate new concepts and acquire new skills with ease, is often puzzling for the learning disabled student. Anxiety and confusion may churn within these children as author/psychotherapist Eileen Simpson so strikingly conveys in her autobiography, *Reversals*.

My brain ached.

_____   _____   _____

Both my teachers accused me of not trying. They had no idea what an effort I was making. Was, saw, was, saw. How were they so sure which it was? . . . Rattled by Auntie's foot tapping, I decided for "saw."

"No, no, NO. How *can* you be so stupid? The word is 'was.' WAS WAS WAS. And for heaven's sake *stop sniveling.*"

_____   _____   _____

I admonished myself to keep calm, to fight the panic, opaque as fog, numbing as ether, which rolled in and settled on my brain.

_____   _____   _____

I was convinced I was defective both intellectually and morally. I was stupid. I was lazy. I was a liar. I was a petty thief. I was an awkward, accident-prone, slovenly, stooped, stuttering, dirty, crybaby.

It wasn't until Ms. Simpson was in graduate school and was given the Wechsler Adult Intelligence Scale that it was found she had a rating of superior intelligence.

Acceptance by Teachers and Peers

Lack of self-confidence may be reinforced by the classmates of the learning disabled child. Being teased, rejected or openly ignored by one's peers further shreds a child's already battered ego. Statistically, children with learning differences rank in the lowest one-third of the mainstream classroom in terms of social acceptance. Social status is conferred by one's classmates based on the criteria of academic achievement, social behavior, and physical appearance (Siperstein and Gottlieb, 1977).

As learning disabled children not infrequently exhibit challenges in both the academic and social domain, their acceptance in the classroom is often undermined. Studies have indicated that although learning disabled children are physically integrated into the mainstream classroom, socially they continue to remain separate. One survey found that 26 percent of these children were isolated or rejected by their peers in comparison to 9 percent of non-learning disabled children (Siperstein and Goding, 1983). Furthermore, it has been ascertained that a significant percentage of mainstreamed children who learn differently suffer a substantial decrease in self-esteem in the regular classroom (Kaplowitz, 1981).

A study by educational researchers, Bryan, Cosden, and Pearl in 1982 documented that rejection and devaluation of the learning disabled child in the classroom is commonly issued not only by the classmates but by the teacher as well. It was found that as early as first grade, teachers offer more negative comments and fewer positive statements to learning disabled students than to those who learn with ease. While offering support and encouragement to the facile learner, teachers sometimes withhold these reinforcers from the child who struggles to learn. Researchers observed that teachers unknowingly make less frequent eye contact, seat children in the distant corners of the class, offer fewer choices of materials and activities, and communicate more critically with the child who experiences problems in learning. Teachers who tend not to engage in negative interactions with learning disabled children in their mainstreamed classes are often inclined rather to ignore them.

These communications on the part of the classroom teacher are not intentional (Good and Brophy, 1974). It has been found that teachers are unaware of the differential quality of their responses and that the unconscious basis for the disparate interactional styles is a distinct and substantial difference in expectations. Teachers tend to anticipate that learning disabled children will behave in an undesirable manner and will be unmotivated and incompetent learners. It is not unusual for educators to view learning disabled students as less desirable class members than non-learning disabled students (Garrett and Crump, 1980; Seaman, 1973) and to perceive these children even more negatively than learning disabled children view themselves (Rosser, 1974).

The impact of low teacher expectation is profound, for it influences not only the student-teacher interactions but the attitude of the classmates toward the learning disabled child. Perhaps more importantly, the teacher's attitude and expectations become adopted by learning disabled children as their own. A significant relationship has been found to exist between children's perceptions of the teacher's expectations and their perception of themselves (Davidson and Lang, 1960). Richardson and Dalton in 1973, found that teacher ratings of academic ability in a child with learning difficulties related to the student's self-concept. Because children tend to respond in the manner anticipated by the teacher, the teacher's influence on a child's performance and his self-perception is powerful.

> Mike, age eleven, visually handicapped and challenged by a decided limp and speech impediment, transferred from public to private school in grade five. A warm, friendly, and sensitive child, Mike announced after three weeks in his new class, "I'm so happy I came to this school." When asked why he felt that way, Mike swallowed hard and whispered, "Because in my old school they called me Dumb Bunny. My teacher used to call me that, and then the kids started to call me Dumb Bunny. They made me feel so stupid."

Educators have an exceptional opportunity to influence the self-esteem of students regardless of their abilities or learning style. Teachers' perceptions may drape students in the shadows of feeble expectations or may lead them to a path of self-discovery where they learn to revel in and stride toward their unique talents, interests, and abilities.

A Classroom Challenge

The skills, talents, imagination, and energy of the classroom teacher are in constant demand in the inclusive classroom, for it is here that educators are challenged to guide and inspire students with widely differing needs, abilities, motivation, and learning styles. Some are gifted, some talented, some struggle to learn, some are neglected or abused at home, some are angry, and others withdrawn, and some are a composite of many of these traits. Is it possible to integrate such a disparate group into a cohesive class while still answering the cries of each child? Can teachers, given the time limitations of the school year, not only offer the requisite academic skills but respond to each youngster's individual needs?

Educators can't do it alone! However, if the energy, talent, and enthusiasm of each student is directed toward a common focus, the synergy created will help to illuminate their paths and light their hearts and minds. The focus is the development of respect on the part of all children for the humanity of their peers while simultaneously guiding individual students to recognize and rejoice in their own unique strengths, interests, and self-efficacy.

CHAPTER 4

The Teacher as Model

The spark must first be lit by the teacher, who serves as a powerful model for the class. If the teacher expresses enthusiasm, sensitivity, and respect for individual differences, and accepts no less from her students, then the class will become a safe and welcome haven. Facial expression, tone of voice, body language, and words combine to communicate acceptance or rejection, and students pattern their own interactions after the instructor's. Bandura and Walters, in their 1963 study, show that students' imitation of their teachers' behaviors merely requires consistency over time.

The teacher's position in the classroom as role model for tolerance and appreciation of individual differences is a potent one. In 1967, educational researcher B. Gallagher found that there exists a profound relationship between teacher attitude and expectations and the response of the class to children with learning differences. When the teacher's attitude was positive rather than neutral or negative, the classmates tended to be more accepting of their learning disabled peers. In numerous studies, data suggest that teachers play a vital role in determining whether children are accepted or rejected in the classroom. Furthermore, when teachers have low expectations for the children who have problems learning in the mainstream, those problems become magnified due to a downward spiral in self-esteem.

Specifically, it behooves educators to establish realistically high expectations for each student, for when little is anticipated, the student's responses reflect the impoverished expectations. If the teacher focuses on the student's difficulties, then the student frequently functions from a position of weakness. However, if the teacher guides each child to identify his personal interests and strengths, the student will likely be excited to learn more about his world and his potential contribution to it.

> Robbie, a seven-year-old gifted student capable of academic work many years above grade level, nevertheless struggled in the classroom. Attentional, motor, and social disorders precipitated behavioral problems in class. He seemed to have no friends and found recess to be the most stressful part of the day.
>
> Robbie's teacher recognized and was excited about his extraordinary potential. She was struck by his intense fascination with architecture, feeling that this just

might be the vehicle to stimulate and challenge Robbie's talents in art, science, and math. The teacher contacted a local children's science museum and proposed a joint venture in which Robbie could participate in an independent study focusing on architecture. Robbie now spends one hour a week during the school day at the museum under the guidance of museum personnel. His enthusiasm, increased self-confidence, and joy in learning have become evident in his calmer, more focused behavior in the classroom. Robbie's peers have responded positively to the changes in his behavior and have begun to include him in their activities.

Encouraging Commitment

Success in establishing a classroom in which self-esteem and sensitivity flourish is in large part dependent on the students' involvement and commitment to these ideals. As models and guides for students, teachers can set forth the basic behavioral expectations of consideration and respect, but it is only when youngsters become personally involved in identifying the acceptable behaviors and classroom rules that this program will come to life. Internalization of these principles will result in greater tolerance for individual differences and a sharp reduction of insensitive words and actions often directed at those most vulnerable. Noted author and psychologist Eda LeShan states in her book *In Search of Myself and Other Children,* "We need to devise school settings in which it is simply not possible for cruelty to be tolerated."

Celebrating Cooperation

A warm, safe, welcoming environment can be created if teachers acknowledge and reinforce desired behaviors in their students. Praising youngsters when cooperation is apparent, when children are sensitive to and supportive of one another, will help to assure that these behaviors will be repeated. Behaviorist B.F. Skinner determined in his work that positive reinforcement is far more effective in instituting behavioral change than is punishment. To be viable, this reinforcement must be in the form of specific rather than general praise so that students are helped to identify the desired behaviors (Weinstein, 1982). Rather than acknowledging student effort with the words, "Good work" or "Fine job," it is far more rewarding for the child to be told exactly which efforts or actions are appreciated. To hear, "Thank you for waiting so patiently" or "I appreciate the way you shared those materials" gives direct cues to the child as to the behavior that is valued.

Rewarding Behavioral Change

For many children, the intrinsic rewards of learning motivate them to remain on task, concentrate, cooperate, and complete assignments. However, some students, particularly those for whom learning is especially challenging, may find that rewards in the form of special events or privileges are personally meaningful. Working to earn these privileges helps to inspire many children to focus on their lessons and exert additional effort in cooperative activities. Guiding the child to identify the specific behaviors to be modified and selecting a desirable reward to be conferred upon achieving those behaviors often enhance behavior management in the classroom. Too, celebrating the development of cooperation, consideration, and academic skills with the entire class can lend an additional sense of joy and anticipation to learning.

The range of positive reinforcers is limitless and need not be costly. Extra story time, recess period, or free time are a few simple but appreciated rewards. Cost-free celebrations such as class picnics or hikes, Toy Day, Stuffed Animal Day or Game Day are highly prized. Parents can be invited to become involved by coming to school to cook with the children or to teach a specific skill. They might be invited to help the children create their own ice cream sundaes in celebration of reaching a specified goal. Utilizing a positive system in acknowledging desired behaviors teaches children that their efforts are honored and that learning can be a joyful experience.

> A grade four class, with the assistance of the teacher, set as a goal for itself respectful listening to one another. They also were to work on making transitions quickly and quietly. Each morning and afternoon the class had an opportunity to earn credit for these cooperative behaviors. As a reward the class chose to have a party organized by the students. The youngsters worked toward these objectives with enthusiasm, reminding each other of the celebration that awaited. Behavior management became considerably more pleasant once the students took responsibility for monitoring their own actions.

Encouraging Peer Support

Development of the classroom as a concerned, supportive community can be fostered when children are encouraged to think of themselves as a *team*, a cohesive unit in which each member is responsible for the well-being of every other student. Children taught to problem solve in a creative, positive fashion are more likely to invest their energies in assisting their peers rather than in denigrating them. Students who are part of a problem-solving team designed to seek workable solutions to difficult situations within the classroom are involved in a process that fosters communication and growth for each of its members.

> Jenny, an attractive, dark haired eight-year-old girl with learning and social disabilities, often came to the resource room in tears crying that no one wanted to be her friend. She'd sob, "I don't know why no one wants to play with me." One

day Jenny announced, "I figured out why the kids never let me play. It's because I'm stupid and ugly."

It was clear that intervention in the classroom was vital. The specialist spoke with the students when Jenny was not in the class. She asked the students to describe Jenny's behavior in the classroom and to delineate particular areas of difficulty. As a team the children were encouraged to think of ways to assist Jenny in developing friendships. They worked cooperatively and enthusiastically in brainstorming suggestions that might prove helpful to Jenny. Some of the children asked if they might come down to the resource room during her recess time to be with her in the special education setting.

In a follow-up session a few weeks later, the class reported that Jenny was now invited to participate in their activities and that she was making excellent progress in getting along. It was evident that the children had become invested in Jenny's success in the mainstream setting, for they proudly related their personal contributions to her adjustment in the classroom. Jenny spoke excitedly about her many new friends.

Vital, too, in encouraging peer respect and support is to assist students in developing an awareness and acceptance of differences in learning style. Children are often relieved to learn that every individual learns differently and has particular areas of strength and weakness. With this insight, students can reflect on their own manner of learning as well as develop an understanding and sensitivity regarding the learning challenges of other students.

Identifying Individual Strengths

If the classroom setting is an accepting and nurturing one, then each child, regardless of learning style or learning difference, will likely begin to identify his or her own talents, abilities, and interests. This is crucial in the establishment of a healthy sense of self-esteem. For when one feels capable, competent, and worthy, that individual is far more likely to succeed in school. The Massachusetts Department of Education's 1989 Position Paper, *Educating the Whole Student: The School's Role in the Physical, Intellectual, Social and Emotional Development of Children,* documents "the dynamic relationship between students' self-esteem, their academic achievement, and their future success in the society."

When teachers and peers assist a child in identifying capabilities and interests, it is then essential that the child be encouraged to actively apply these abilities in the school setting. Talent in art can be utilized to enhance the appearance of the classroom, halls, and offices. Musical ability can be highlighted to provide pleasure not only during designated music time but during class productions or simply during break time.

Randy, a ten-year-old girl with a history of learning and language difficulties, was withdrawn and school phobic. During her third grade year, Randy revealed that she loved to dance and often worked on dance routines at home. Her special class organized an "Oldies but Goodies" presentation to be performed for the mainstream classes and parents and friends. Randy's joy as she worked on choreographing a dance for the show was contagious. Each morning she came to school with innovations for her performance. Her face shown with anticipation, and when volunteers were requested to be the master of ceremony, Randy's hand shot up. The day of the performance this child, who had a history of stuttering, introduced the program flawlessly. The cheers from the audience were as genuine as the pride that shown in Randy's eyes. She was a star.

Children who enjoy and excel in any of the academic skills can become peer tutors for their classmates or younger children. In the guide *Improving Social Competence: Techniques for Teachers,* peer tutoring is advocated as a means of improving social and academic functioning, enhancing self-esteem, as well as increasing positive attitudes toward school and learning. Students can be encouraged to advertise their talents on the bulletin board and offer to assist others interested in learning or practicing a new skill. Reaching out to others and establishing connections offers a powerful motivation to invest one's self in school.

Ted, an imaginative ten year old who was a fluent and voracious reader, experienced severe Attention Deficit Disorder. Not only did it affect school progress, it impinged on social development as well. As reading provided both solace and pleasure for Ted, it was decided to use this as an avenue to build his self-esteem. He was invited to be a "big brother" to a young boy who has Down Syndrome who attended class in the same school. Ted's responsibility each week was to take his "little brother" to the library to select a special book. Ted would then read to the child and then walk him back to class. Both children treasured their time together. Ted's sense of responsibility and pride in himself grew as the year progressed. His enhanced self-regard was evident in straighter posture, improved eye contact, and a stronger voice. He knew that he was important.

The Teacher's Impact

Teachers, through the power of expectations and communication, exert an influence on students that may be lifelong. Julius Segal, PhD, psychologist, author, and lecturer, wrote in the Brown University Child Behavior and Development Letter of the profound impact that teachers have on the future of children in their classes. As significant persons in our students' world, teachers do have the power to touch the lives of each one, particularly those who are most in need. Resilient youngsters who surmount trauma in the home or overcome academic or social conflicts often do so as a result of the "presence in their lives of a charismatic adult—a person with whom they identify and from whom they gather strength. In a surprising number of cases, that person turns out to be a teacher." Dr. Segal goes on to say, "Teachers often provide the magical bond that allows many children to turn their lives from certain defeat to glorious victory."

> Nancy was born out of wedlock to a woman who gave birth to her second child in a prison hospital. As a young girl, Nancy's mother took her to bars where she was introduced as the woman's little sister. Growing up, Nancy was taunted by neighborhood children. She heard repeatedly, "You're gonna be just like your mama." In fourth grade, Nancy had a teacher who recognized her quick mind and sensitive nature. He supported, encouraged, and challenged her, filling Nancy with a belief in her own power to shape her future. Nancy began to set goals and achieve them. Today she is a child development specialist and college professor.

Teachers inspire through a steadfast belief in the integrity and capabilities of each student. The desire to learn, to grow, to be strong can be fueled in the classroom as students are led to the path of self-acceptance, self-appreciation, and self-respect. Teachers hold aloft the beacon that lights the children's way to finding their own special selves. Teachers do make a difference!

Teaching Consideration and Respect
in the Classroom

Theme I

Making a Difference

Theme II

Establishing Behavioral Expectations

Theme III

Developing Sensitivity Toward Others

Theme IV

Encouraging Supportive Classroom Behaviors

Theme V

Developing Positive Visualization & Self-Talk Strategies

Theme VI

Building Self-Esteem

Theme VII

Understanding & Respecting Variations in Learning Style

Theme VIII

Considering Those Who Learn Differently

Theme IX

The Classroom as a Team

Making a Difference

Purpose

To introduce self-discovery, self-acceptance, and personal and social responsibility.

Objectives

The student will be able to:

1. Acknowledge individual responsibility to influence the direction of one's own life.
2. Become aware of one's potential to enhance the quality of the lives of others.
3. Be receptive to the exploration of individual styles of learning, thinking, creating, and relating.

Presentation Suggestions

Introduction

How many of you have thought about traveling into outer space, journeying by rocket to explore our expansive universe? Today we are going to embark upon a journey that is even more important and fascinating. Today we will begin our travel to inner space.

Class Discussion

a. Where is inner space?
b. Inner space is inside each one of us. It is what makes us special and different from anyone else. It is made up of our thoughts and feelings and interests and abilities. Over the next several weeks we will explore our own inner space, our own personal universe. You will each begin a journey, one that will hopefully last a lifetime, to discover what

it means to be you. You will explore how you think and learn and what is important to you. You will discover your own skills and talents and those activities that are especially meaningful and exciting to you. And, you will learn about the power you have to guide your own life and help other people.

c. We call this journey *I Make a Difference!*

d. Write the words *I Make a Difference!* on the board or on a chart and keep these words visible for the class for the duration of the unit.

e. Ask the children to say the words *I Make a Difference!* with you. Have them repeat these words at the beginning of each of the unit sessions.

Activities

a. Request that the students draw a picture and/or write a description of a special way in which they have made a difference either in their own lives, in their families, in school, in the life of a pet, a friend, in the community, etc. Ask the children to consider how they as individuals made a positive difference because of something they said or did.

b. Have the children discuss their contributions in small groups of four or five children. Encourage them to ask one another questions after their individual presentations.

Establishing Behavioral Expectations

Purpose

To present *consideration* and *respect* as cornerstones of classroom behavior.

Objectives

The student will be able to:

1. Explain the meaning of consideration and respect.
2. Delineate specific behaviors exemplifying consideration and respect in the classroom.

Presentation Suggestions

Introduction

As in any journey, when we travel we have to be certain that we are safe. When astronauts travel to outer space, how do they protect themselves? We need to be certain that in our journey to inner space we create a classroom that provides us with a safe and comfortable environment. In this classroom we need to feel free to learn, to explore, and to express ourselves without fear that others will laugh or tease. We need to protect ourselves and each other.

We will call the process we use C.A.R.E.
- Write the acronym on the board.
- Each letter stands for a word.
- C = Consider, A = And, R = Respect, E = Everyone

Discussion Questions

a. What does the word *consider* mean? Discuss the meaning of the word and request examples of considerate behavior.

b. What does the word *respect* mean? (Repeat above discussion.)

c. Do you believe that it matters whether or not people show consideration and respect in the classroom? Why?

d. What would our classroom be like if people did not behave with consideration and respect?

e. How would it affect our feelings? How would it affect our learning?

f. What would our classroom be like if there were no rules?

g. Would you enjoy being a student in a class where there were no rules? Why do you feel this way?

h. Are students the only people who have to follow rules? Where else are rules important?

Small Group Activity

Students and teacher will brainstorm expectations for classroom behavior designed to establish a safe and respectful learning environment. This activity may be performed as a whole class or in small groups. Children working cooperatively in small groups should submit their ideas to be incorporated into a master list. The final list of rules should be brief, attainable, and phrased in a positive fashion. Example: *Speak politely* rather than *no rudeness*.

Concluding Questions/Suggestions

a. In following these rules will we, as class members, consider and respect everyone? How will the rules help us?

b. Discuss the classroom procedures and the consequences should the rules be honored or ignored. Will there be a reminder, a warning, etc., if the students fail to follow the rules? Will there be a reward or celebration when the students meet the expectations for a given period of time?

c. Display the rules beneath a C.A.R.E. sign in a location that can be easily viewed.

d. Routinely review the expectations with the class to help the students internalize them.

e. Rephrase the rules periodically to help keep the expectations meaningful and viable.

Developing Sensitivity Toward Others

Purpose

To raise awareness of the effect of our actions on the feelings of others.

Objectives

The student will be able to:

1. Empathize with the pride, satisfaction, joy, anger or hurt of others.
2. Become aware of the common needs of all people.

Presentation Suggestions

Introduction

The letters C.A.R.E., which stand for Consider and Respect Everyone, are really only letters. They are not magical and by themselves have no real meaning. How do these letters, which spell the word CARE, acquire meaning? (Discuss with the class one's own responsibility to give life to these letters.)

How have you in the past weeks shown consideration and respect to someone either in this class or outside of it? You may have been particularly helpful or thoughtful during lessons, recess, special subjects, at play or in the community. (Discuss with your students examples of your own contributions to the well-being of others to serve as an example of the types of activities that demonstrate consideration and respect.)

Class Discussion and Activities

a. Ask the students to discuss, write or draw pictures exploring their recent experiences regarding consideration and respect of others.

b. How did you feel when you assisted someone else? How did the other person feel? How do you know?

c. Let's make a list describing persons you feel deserve our consideration and respect. (This may be done as a cooperative learning project.) Why do you feel they deserve our respect?

d. What if people are different from you in the way they look, think or act? Do they deserve your consideration? Why?

e. In what ways are people, although they are different, all alike? What do all people need to survive and be happy?

f. Do you believe that a new baby who doesn't understand language deserves to be treated with respect? Why?

g. How is respect shown to an infant?

h. Discuss the German experiment of the early 13th century designed by Emperor Frederick II. The emperor wished to determine the language and style of speech that would develop in children who had never heard the spoken word. He forbade caretakers in an orphanage to speak to the babies or to give them any but the minimal care. They only were allowed to hastily feed, bathe, and change them without any show of affection or attention. Tragically, the experiment ended in failure, for all of the babies died (Montagu, 1971).

i. Imagine a child who, because of a severe handicap, could neither see, nor hear, nor speak. Some children whose mothers had German measles while they were pregnant were born deaf and blind. Does it matter whether such a child were to be shown consideration and respect? Why would it matter? In what ways could you show consideration and respect to a person who could neither see nor hear?

j. Show the videotape "The Miracle Worker," the story of the life of Helen Keller, or have the children read a biography or autobiography about Ms. Keller.

Discuss Helen's handicaps, talents, and the role her teacher Anne Sullivan played in changing her life.

Were Anne Sullivan's expectations of Helen realistic? If her teacher had allowed Helen to continue behaving in the way she had in the past, how would Helen's life have been different?

k. Have any of you had experiences with elderly people? What have you done to show older people special consideration and respect?

l. What is it called when people of different races or religions are discriminated against? How do you suppose it feels?

m. Discuss the subject of prejudice and its negative effects on the individual and society.

Follow-Up Activities

a. Ask the students to work in small groups to design and present projects to the class that will give insight into various challenges which individuals may face. Group projects on prejudice, abuse, handicapping conditions, aging, homeless, etc., can help the students gain insight and sensitivity toward those who are perceived as being different from one's self. The projects may be in the form of a skit, research presentation, panel discussion, interview, etc. (Feedback from students in a grade five class participating in this program indicated that this activity was one of the most valuable and memorable experiences of the *I Make a Difference!* program.)

b. Explore community service opportunities that would encourage students to assist the elderly, handicapped individuals, the homeless, etc., either through fund raising or direct service. Adopt a class community service project that would require planning, cooperation, organization, and implementation.

c. Design a personal C.A.R.E. card to be placed in a notebook that would serve as a reminder to consider and respect everyone. The card should be decorated with the words "I C.A.R.E. I Make a Difference!"

Encouraging Supportive Classroom Behaviors

Purpose

To decrease the tendency in students to tease, reject or ignore their peers.

Objectives

The student will be able to:

1. Communicate in written, artistic or dramatic expression the consequences of teasing.
2. Understand the motivation for teasing.
3. Develop healthy coping mechanisms in response to hurtful behaviors.

Presentation Suggestions

Introduction

When classmates don't treat each other with consideration and respect, how do they sometimes behave toward one another? (Tease, reject, ignore)

How does it feel to be teased? Nearly everyone has had the experience of being teased, rejected or ignored by other children. (The teacher is encouraged to share personal experiences.)

Activity

Ask the children to write a description of an occasion when they might have been teased. They may also draw or write about observing such a situation as long as the people mentioned are not in the class. Assure the children that this is a private activity and that it need not be handed in. If, however, any students would like to share, they are encouraged to do so.

Discussion Questions

a. Why do you think people tease? (Feel poorly about selves, personal problems, enjoy seeing others upset, desire to feel superior.)

b. Is teasing acceptable? Why or why not?

c. What is the best way to respond to teasing? (Ignore, tell an adult, express your displeasure at the comment.)

d. Can we guarantee that other people will not tease us?

e. Although teasing is not acceptable behavior, it does sometimes occur. If in spite of your best efforts it continues, what should you do to help yourself cope? (Guide the children to realize that believing in themselves, being aware of their strengths, and respecting their abilities is often the best protection.

Concluding Activities

a. Imagine that a younger child comes to you for help because he or she is being teased. This child might be a brother, sister, cousin, younger friend or even yourself when you were little. Write a description or draw a picture of the situation that is troubling the child. Tell of your relationship to the child and of the advice that you gave to him or her.

b. After the papers are written, tell the students to picture the child returning to say that the teasing has not stopped. What further advice would you give to the young child?

c. In groups of 3, 4, or 5, have the children construct skits to portray the pain of teasing. Have the children resolve the conflict in a positive manner.

Developing Positive Visualization and Self-Talk Strategies

Purpose

To guide students to visualize and pursue positive goals.

Objectives

The student will be able to:

1. Identify traits and characteristics that led people who struggled to ultimately succeed in their objectives.

2. Become aware of the impact of one's attitude on direction, performance, and satisfaction.

3. Recognize the power of visualization and positive self-talk strategies in achieving one's goals.

4. Become cognizant of one's responsibilities to make a difference in one's own future.

Presentation Suggestions

Introduction

We have learned about the struggles that Helen Keller overcame to become a student, writer, lecturer, and model of strength and courage for people all over the world.

How did she accomplish these successes?

Encourage the children to explore the role of her family and teacher, yet guide them to recognize that it was her own determination that primarily accounted for her remarkable successes.

Discussion Questions

a. Would Helen Keller's life have been different if Helen, in spite of the support of the important people in her life, hadn't believed in herself? What if she were convinced that because of her blindness and deafness she would never be able to speak or write or learn?

b. Do you think that her confidence played a role in her achievements? In what way?

c. Although Helen was blind, do you think that she could see herself achieving her goals of becoming a strong student, a writer, and world famous speaker? How could she picture this in spite of her blindness? (Assist the students to understand that visualization is a mental picture and an extremely powerful form of suggestion. Explain that successful athletes, such as those in the Olympics, use this method to improve their performance.)

Visualization and Self-Talk Procedures

a. Encourage the children to visualize themselves achieving a goal that is important to them. Have them close their eyes and see themselves performing an activity that they would like to master. Help them understand that consistently seeing themselves performing well or accomplishing their goals will bring them toward achievement.

b. In addition to picturing success, what do you think Helen did to help herself overcome her extreme handicaps?

c. Discuss positive self-talk and the influence that Helen exerted by speaking to herself in an encouraging, determined manner.

d. Teach the children how to speak to themselves positively. Explain that if they repeatedly say phrases such as, "I am a powerful runner" or "I write exciting stories" or "I will be a scientist," they will powerfully assist themselves toward achieving those goals. The book *I Think I Can. I Know I Can* by Susan Isaacs and Wendy Ritchey is an excellent reference for teachers.

e. Introduce the acronym *S.S.S.* to signify the expression *See and Say Success*.

f. Helen Keller once wrote, "There is no valley so deep and dark but a path leads up from it to the light."

   What does this statement mean to you? How might belief that we can climb from the darkness of life's problems up toward the light make it so?

g. Encourage the children to recognize that *S.S.S.* will result in powerful actions that will alter the course of one's life.

Activities

a. Draw or write a description about your own "valley" or time of struggle or about a problem that confronted someone close to you. Explain how *See and Say Success* altered the outcome of this challenge. Explore how you made a difference in what might have happened.

b. Everyone in life experiences difficulties, some of which may seem overwhelming. I am going to read descriptions of the challenges faced by some very famous people, and I would like you to guess who these people may be. Because of their own *S.S.S.* they overcame their hardships and lived remarkable and successful lives.

● **Case I:** This child did not speak in full sentences until he was four years old. When he was in elementary school, he had many problems in learning, especially in reading. He was not thought to be a good student, and his teachers often criticized him. This boy was poor at sports and thought that playing games was silly. He had no friends. As a child he made up his own religion and talked to himself. Even his own father had a difficult time accepting him.

(The child was Albert Einstein.)

● **Case II:** When this baby was born, he had a very large head and looked strange. His doctor believed that he had a brain disease. Relatives and neighbors thought that he was strange, and his teacher, because of his great difficulty in math, thought that he was dumb. The teacher told his mother that her son's brains were all mixed up. His mother taught him at home.

(The child was Thomas Edison.)

● **Case III:** This baby was born to extremely poor parents. One side of his face was paralyzed, and when he grew older and went to school the other kids teased him and called him "slant mouth." He was a straight D student. His father constantly told him that he didn't have a brain. This boy was always creating problems, getting thrown out of school, and running away from home.

(The child was Sylvester Stallone.)

Follow-Up Activities

a. Assign biographies and autobiographies of famous people who struggled due to personal hardships, prejudice or alignment with unpopular causes. Suggest that the students present book projects with themselves taking on the persona of the subject of the book. Speaking in the first person, in costume if possible, encourage each student to discuss the personal challenges, attitudes, goals, and ultimate successes of the individual. Verbalize the positive images and messages that the subject gave to himself. After each presentation, encourage the class to discuss how this person's life would have been different if not for the ability to *See and Say Success.*

Possible subjects of books may include: Hans Christian Anderson, Ludwig van Beethoven, Elizabeth Blackwell, Louis Braille, Laura Bridgeman, Winston Churchill, Tom Cruise, Thomas Edison, Albert Einstein, Bruce Jenner, Martin Luther King, Jr., Abraham Lincoln, Greg Louganis, Amy Lowell, Rosa Parks, Jackie Robinson, Nelson Rockefeller, Eleanor Roosevelt, August Rodin, Sylvester Stallone, Anne Sullivan, Harriet Tubman, Booker T. Washington, Henry Winkler, and Stevie Wonder.

b. Invite as classroom speakers successful people from the community who would like to share an account of their own struggles and methods for overcoming them. Consider inviting people with various handicapping conditions to relate their strategies for coping with personal challenges. Also invite people who became successful in fields that require remarkable perseverance.

c. Ask the children to write a letter addressed to you and written as though they were twenty-two years of age. Have them tell you of their interests, experiences, goals, and accomplishments as well as any special challenges that they may have met and overcome. Instruct the children to describe in their letter the power of *S.S.S.* in helping them to achieve their own successes. Ask them to consider how they made a difference in their own lives.

Building Self-Esteem

Purpose

To assist students in establishing or expanding their sense of self-worth and competence.

Objectives

The student will be able to:

1. Identify personal abilities, strengths, and interests.
2. Perceive themselves to be capable and worthwhile individuals.
3. Recognize ways in which they make a difference in the lives of others.

Presentation Suggestions

Introduction

When we learned about *See and Say Success,* we discovered that people who think positively about themselves tend to achieve more of their dreams and goals.

What do you think successful people believe about themselves?

Guide the students to understand that liking one's self and possessing self-respect are indicators of high self-esteem.

How do positive pictures and words that people see and hear in their own minds assist them in achieving their goals?

Discussion Questions

a. Do you believe that it is important for you to like yourself?

   Discuss the relationship of high self-esteem to the belief that one can accomplish one's goals even in the face of adversity or negative peer pressure.

b. Is liking yourself the same as being conceited? What is the difference?

c. How do you think people learn to like themselves?

   Discuss the role of feedback from others as well as appreciation of one's abilities and pride in accomplishments in the development of self-esteem.

d. Consider the people we read about who accomplished their goals and changed the world for the better. If they hadn't had high self-esteem, do you think that their lives would have made a difference in ours?

e. If these successful people hadn't believed in themselves, what might they have said to themselves when their lives became difficult?

   Further explore the concept of self-talk. Discuss the dangers of negative self-talk, e.g., "I'm dumb, I'm ugly, I'm unpopular, I can't do anything right," etc., and its impact on a person's self-esteem and ability to act. Compare the feelings and sensations one experiences when saying "I can" vs. saying "I can't."

f. What do you think these remarkable people told themselves to help them climb out of their personal valleys to find a more positive path?

Activities

a. These well known people were young once, just like you. They had to learn about their talents and interests to help them speak positively about themselves to themselves.

   You are going to have a chance to discover your special abilities and interests and learn to speak to yourself in kind, positive, and encouraging ways.

   We each have personal skills and talents that make us unique. These abilities often lead to fascination with particular topics, activities, and hobbies.

   Give each student a large sheet of construction paper and the following directions:

   1. Write your name in bold letters in the middle of the paper.

   2. Around your name draw or write the names of activities that give you special pleasure. These activities should be related to all areas of your life: school, home, sports, clubs, friends, etc.

   3. Share your papers in small discussion groups and ask questions of each

other regarding your personal interests.

This activity gives the students a chance not only to identify their own areas of interests and abilities but to help classmates learn more about one another.

b. Students draw or bring in small pictures of themselves and paste the picture in the middle of a heart. Around the heart the students draw or write reasons why they like and respect themselves.

c. During the course of the school year, on birthdays or other special occasions, each student should have the opportunity to sit as part of a classroom circle and listen to the ways in which classmates think he or she is special.

Follow-Up Activities

a. All of us make a difference in the lives of other people. Many times we don't even think about the many ways in which we help other people in our community lead better, happier lives.

Give the students an example of how you, as an adult, teacher, friend, and community member, make a difference in the lives of others.

b. Ask each student to write and illustrate a book entitled "I Make a Difference!" devoted to exploring the many ways in which the child makes a difference. Each page could refer to a specific activity or relationship. Upon completion, these books can be shared with one another either in small groups or in front of the class.

c. Students can place advertisements on the bulletin board offering to teach other children a particular skill or game.

d. Write or illustrate ways in which you would like to make a difference in the lives of others when you are grown.

—

Understanding and Respecting Variations in Learning Style

Purpose

To develop an awareness and appreciation for individual differences in styles of learning.

Objectives

The student will be able to:

1. Describe the function of the visual, auditory, and kinesthetic modes of learning.
2. Comprehend that each person possesses a unique learning style based on individual brain organization.
3. Identify his or her own learning style preferences.

Presentation Suggestions

Introduction

Each of you made a chart with your name in the center, and around your name you drew pictures or wrote descriptions of activities that you especially enjoy.

Was your chart exactly like anyone else's in your group? Do you think that it would be precisely like anyone else's in the class? In the school? In your family? In the state? In the country? Do you suppose that you are exactly like anyone else in the world?

If you had an identical twin, would you be alike in every way? Would your every thought be identical? Do you think that you would both want to do the same things, eat the same food, play the same games, be with the same people at every moment of every day?

Do you think there is anyone exactly like you in this entire world? Why not?

Guide the children to consider that everyone's brain and experiences are different, and therefore we each have our own interests, talents, and personality.

Read to the class the book *My Three Uncles* by Yossi Abolafia, published by Greenwillow Books, New York, 1985. It is a story about identical triplets whose young niece struggles to tell them apart. Direct the class to be detectives and to listen for clues that might help the girl identify her uncles. Humorous differences in interests and personality become apparent. Some of the children might wish to take notes.

Discussion Questions

a. The triplets looked identical and were raised in the same home, yet were they alike in every way?

b. How were they different?

c. Why do you think they were different?

   The following discussion explains the fact that each person's brain is unique in terms of cellular, electrical, and chemical makeup.

d. Each of us has a brain that is uniquely ours. It is like no one else's. Did you know that our brains are made up of billions of nerve cells that fit together like a puzzle? Everyone's brain puzzle is slightly different, just the way everyone's fingerprints are slightly different. These brain cells send messages through electrical and chemical signals. The electricity that flows from cell to cell moves at a slightly different rate and direction in each brain. Also, each person's brain chemistry is slightly different. It is in part because our brains are organized differently that our interests, talents, personality, and style of learning are special in each one of us.

e. Do you think that life would be different if everyone's brain was exactly like everyone else's? What might the world be like if each person's brain cells, brain chemistry, and electrical signals were identical?

f. Would you be pleased to live in a world in which everyone's thoughts and feelings and abilities were exactly alike?

Activities

a. Pretend that you have an identical twin. Not even your best friend can tell you apart. Imagine that your friend is invited to spend the night and that you and your twin switch beds during the night. In the morning your friend thinks that you are your twin and your twin is you. As the morning progresses, your friend becomes suspicious because certain habits of yours give you away.

Write a list describing your morning behavior, attitudes, and routines from the time you awake until you are ready to leave the house.

b. We are all familiar with heart transplants, lung transplants, and kidney transplants. Do you think that brain transplants would be a good idea?

Pretend that you and a partner have volunteered for an experimental brain exchange designed to help doctors perfect brain transplants. Get together with your brain buddy and find out what you would be like when you awaken from your operation.

Pairs of children will act out visits to one another's homes after the brain exchange.

Discussion of Learning Styles

a. Because our brains are different electrically, chemically, and in cell structure from everyone else's, we each have our own special way of learning. Each of us have things that come easily to us and other things that are more challenging, more difficult.

Discuss with your students some things that are easy and pleasant for you to do and other activities that you find to be more difficult.

b. What are some activities that are especially comfortable for you? What are some that are more difficult?

c. Because our brains are different, we each have our own special talents and skills that usually fit with the way we like to learn. The way we are most comfortable learning is called our learning style. Some people learn best by using their *eyes,* by looking and remembering. These are people who like to watch videotapes, filmstrips, and see pictures when they learn new things.

d. Some people learn best by using their *ears* and remembering what they hear. These students really enjoy listening to stories and may be especially fond of music. People who learn best by using their ears may be great at remembering directions and can often recall names and numbers after hearing them just once.

e. There are people who learn best by using their *hands* or *bodies.* These students often love to build models, do puzzles, enjoy art activities, and like to learn by doing rather than watching or listening.

f. Each of us will now fill out a Learning Style Preference Survey to help us become more aware of how we like to learn. It will help us consider whether we learn best by using our eyes, ears, hands, or a combination of these styles. (Appendix B, page 69)

g. You are going to design two schools on opposite sides of a piece of construction paper.

On one side draw a school that you would especially like to attend because the school specializes in teaching the subject you most enjoy. On the other side of the paper draw a school that you would not choose to attend because it specializes in the subject that you like least. (The children can share and discuss these projects in small groups.)

Considering Those Who Learn Differently

Purpose

To refine an understanding of one's own learning style while developing empathy for those who experience learning challenges.

Objectives

The student will be able to:

1. Develop an understanding of one's own personal learning style through participation in simulations of learning challenges.

2. Achieve acceptance and appreciation of one's own learning style.

3. Become sensitive to the frustrations of those who experience compromises in learning.

   Note: This theme attempts to highlight information about learning styles and learning difficulties through discussion and simulations of learning challenges. During the pilot project, students exhibited an intense interest in discovering their own styles of learning. In gaining an understanding that each person learns in a unique fashion, the students displayed a deeper compassion and sensitivity toward those who struggled in school. The students who are learning disabled were then free to become more open in sharing their feelings and frustrations. Enhanced understanding, communication, and empathy were the results.

   An outstanding teacher and student reference to learning abilities and learning disorders is the book, *Keeping a Head in School* by Mel Levine, MD. Dr. Levine clearly and sensitively explains learning styles and learning struggles to children ages nine to fifteen. Attention, memory, brain function, and social relationships are thoughtfully explored.

   In presenting the simulations to the class, teachers may select a sampling or may choose to employ all of the learning challenges. Where appropriate, the designs found in the appendices may be converted to transparencies for use on the overhead projector.

Presentation Suggestions

In our study of successful people who have overcome challenges to reach their goals, we have learned that many of them experienced severe problems in school. The world's most famous physicist, Albert Einstein, had great difficulty in the classroom. His teacher said of him, "Albert is a very poor student. He is mentally slow, unsociable, and is always daydreaming. He is spoiling it for the rest of the class. It would be in the best interests of all if he were removed from school at once" (McGinnis, 1990).

Thomas Edison, a famous scientist with more than 1,000 inventions, had trouble adding and subtracting when he was a child. An elementary school teacher told the principal that young Thomas's brains were "addled" and that he should not waste his time nor the teacher's time by attending school. At seven years of age Thomas's mother began to teach him at home. This child grew up to be the inventor of the light bulb and the movie projector.

Hans Christian Anderson, the author of *The Ugly Duckling,* struggled to spell, read, and write. When you read the story of the lonely little bird who was teased and tormented by the ducks in the pond, you are really hearing the cry of young Hans. Albert Einstein, Thomas Edison, and Hans Christian Anderson were intelligent, creative, and sensitive people who struggled in school. Their classmates and sometimes their teachers ridiculed them because of their learning problems.

(It is suggested that the children view the videotape Gifts of Greatness, *which explores the lives and learning frustrations of each of these individuals in an entertaining and insightful fashion. See References for more information.)*

How do you think these people felt when they were called names in school? Many children share the learning problems experienced by Edison, Einstein, and Anderson. The students are bright and imaginative but may have difficulty in reading, math, spelling, writing, listening, speaking or making friends. Their diffficulties are related to the way their brains receive and send messages. The signals sent to and from their eyes, ears, hands, and feet may be confused. This confusion may cause problems in paying attention, remembering or communicating. These very frustrating difficulties are not caused by laziness or lack of trying but are a result of mixed up messages in the brain. These problems are sometimes called learning disabilities or learning differences. These same children, although they may have some learning difficulties, may also be especially talented in art, music, sports, science, computers or other areas. Many of today's most famous and successful people had major problems in school. The Olympic athletes Bruce Jenner and Greg Louganis had severe reading problems. Singer and actress Cher and actress and comedienne Whoopi Goldberg had difficulty in spelling and writing when they were children. Tom Cruise and Sylvester Stallone, well known actors, also struggled when they were in the classroom. People teased and called them names because of their learning differences.

We are going to participate in some activities that will help us understand how people may feel when they have problems in learning. In performing these challenges we will sense some of the frustration experienced when people struggle to read, spell, write or follow directions.

Also, these activities will help us determine the ways in which we learn most comfortably. We will explore each of our learning channels: the visual channel, the auditory channel, and the movement channel. These experiments will also help each of us to recognize our strongest channels and our own favorite way of learning.

Visual Simulation Activities

a. The first channel we will explore will be the visual channel. When we take in information through our eyes, we use this channel. We are not however talking about how well we see but how our brain *interprets* what we see.

b. Stare at this design. What do you see? (Appendix C, Vase and Profiles, page 71)

c. Stare also at this design. What do you see? (Appendix D, White and Black Crosses, page 73)

d. Can you force your brain to see only one design in each picture? The designs you see are your brain's interpretation of the picture. Trying to force yourself to see just one picture is impossible because your brain automatically interprets the information without your thinking about it.

e. There are many people whose brains interpret numbers and letters as being reversed. They may see M's as W's and b's as d's. The number 19 may look like 91. The word *did* may look like *bib* or the word *was* may look like *saw*.

f. How do you imagine it feels to read or write when your brain interprets letters and numbers to be in different positions or directions? A person's intelligence is not related to the way his or her brain interprets letters and numbers. Difficulty in reading, which is called dyslexia or a reading disability, is not related to intelligence. Dyslexic people are smart. Their brains may interpret the letters and numbers differently. But, as we shall see, there are many different reasons that a bright person may experience confusion in reading, spelling, math or writing.

g. Ask the students how many ways the word *bad* might be perceived by someone who has reversal problems. (bad, dad, dab, bab. Still other children might perceive it as add, abd, or abb.)

h.   Some people have difficulty in interpreting or perceiving slight differences in letters. The letters h and n are very similar. Lower case n and r are also similar. (Write these letters on the board.) The brain's interpretation of slight differences between letters is called visual discrimination. Students who have difficulty in visual discrimination might interpret the word *rap* to look like *nap* or *fur* to look like *fun*. People who have problems with both letter reversals and visual discrimination might perceive the word *brand* to look like *barhb*.

i.   A visual discrimination challenge will be presented to you. You will have one minute to find the numbered box which is *different* from the sample above. (Appendix E, Page 75)

j.   Prearrange to have a child leave the room as you are completing activity i.

k.   Some of us have remarkable visual memories and recall nearly everything we see. Others of us don't remember details as sharply. One of your friends left the room during our last activity. Let's try to recall what _____ is wearing today.

l.   People with outstanding visual memories tend to remember spelling words rather easily. I'm going to show you a design that might be a spelling word in an alien society. I'll give you six seconds to look at it, and then after a brief pause I shall ask you to write the word. (Appendix F, page 77)

Some people just naturally remember spelling words more easily than others because the portion of their brain responsible for visual memory is especially strong.

m.   This is a picture (Appendix G, page 79) of a note left on the blackboard by a very intelligent fourth grader. What do you think his problems were?

This student had difficulty with visual memory causing him to spell *been* as *bin* and *here* as *hear*. He couldn't remember the way the word looked so instead spelled by using letter sounds. He is what we call an auditory learner. He learns best by using his hearing.

Auditory Simulation Activities

a.   Now we are going to explore our auditory channel, the pathway that receives information through our ears. We are not speaking about how well we hear but about how our brain interprets and remembers the information coming through our ears.

b.   Just as our brains must discriminate fine differences in what we see in order to help us read, our brains must discriminate fine differences in what we hear to help us use sounds in reading, spelling, and understanding. For example, if I said, "Give the disk in your desk to Dick," and you heard "Give the deck in your disk to Dick," could you do what I requested? How do you think problems in auditory discrimination would affect a student who is trying to read, spell, and follow directions? How would it feel to have to cope with this problem day after day in the classroom?

c. We are going to experiment with auditory discrimination. Close your eyes. After I say each pair of words, open them and write down whether the words are the same or different.

> taksabter - taksibter
> flogsdodum - flogsdodum
> higershan - higersham
> snaperdugle - snaberdugle

This activity will help the children evaluate their own ability to discriminate auditorially.

d. Some people have great problems in screening out noises. This problem might make concentrating very difficult. Close your eyes and listen to all the sounds that you hear in the classroom. Do you hear some sounds that you were unaware of before? There are people who are constantly aware of nearly every sound, and this causes problems when they try to do their work in class. The extra noises are not screened out in their brains. When would being super alert to sounds be especially helpful? (For hunters in the woods or when playing hide and seek.)

e. Now I am going to play a song that is very popular. But I don't want you to pay attention to the song. Instead I want you to listen to a description of the game of lacrosse which I will read as the song is playing. I will then ask you questions about the game. (Select a song that you know the children especially enjoy, perhaps a rap song or one with a particularly strong beat. Perhaps you can ask a child to bring in a tape or a record.) The reading is meant to be done in a monotone with the song playing at the same volume.

Read the following passage and ask the children to write down their answers to the questions that you will ask.

Lacrosse—An American Contact Sport

The game of lacrosse is played on a field that is 110 yards long and sixty yards wide. Each of the two goals is six feet high and six feet wide. The goals are placed near the end boundaries of the field and are 80 yards apart. A circle that is 18 feet in diameter and called a crease is marked around the center of each goal line. The only players allowed to enter this area without carrying a ball are the goalkeeper and defensemen. There are ten players on each side, three defensemen, three midfielders, and three attackmen as well as the goalie. At the beginning of play the defensemen are found near their goal while the midfielders spread near the center of the field. The attackmen play in the area of the opponent's goal. Using their sticks, players are allowed to throw, bat, or carry the ball. They are also allowed to kick it. The goalie is the only one who may touch the ball with his hand, but he is not allowed to catch it. The object of the game is to ram or bounce or loft a white or orange India rubber ball weighing five ounces and measuring eight inches in circumference into the opposing goal. Of course, the teams try to keep their opponents from doing the same thing.

1. What are the dimensions of the playing field? (110 by 60)

2. What is the name of the circle around the center of each goal line? (crease)

3. Who are the ten players on each team? (3 defensemen, 3 midfielders, 3 attackmen, goalie)

4. What are the players allowed to do with their sticks? (throw, bat, or carry the ball)

5. Describe the lacrosse ball. (white or orange rubber ball, 5 ounces, 8 inches in circumference)

Do you understand how problems in concentrating can interfere with a person's ability to remember what he or she hears?

Simulations in the Movement or Motor Channel

a. Some people especially like to learn by using movement. These students enjoy using their hands, their feet, their entire bodies to help them understand and remember. Putting on plays, doing experiments, designing solutions are especially important to many students. There are people who enjoy learning by using their bodies but who may experience some difficulty in movement areas such as in handwriting or in coordination. Problems in these areas are not related to intelligence or concentration. These difficulties may occur when faulty messages are flashed between the brain, the eyes, the hands, and the feet.

b. You are going to be given a written challenge requiring your eyes and hands to work together. You have 90 seconds to copy this design. (Appendix H, page 81)

c. In this activity you will have a chance to use the auditory, visual, and movement channels all at the same time. You will be selecting a partner and standing back to back. One of you will be handed a design and will give a description of that design to your partner. The partner who is listening to the description will draw the design as it is being described. The describer may not look at the picture as it is being drawn nor may the drawer see the picture his partner is holding. The drawer may ask questions of the describer regarding confusing details. You will have five minutes for this activity, and then you may look at the original and compare the designs. (Be certain that the student who is drawing cannot see anyone else's sheet. Assure them that there are different designs being used.) (Appendix I-1, I-2, pages 83 & 85)

d. After five minutes have the children compare the original design to the design drawn.

What was it like trying to follow the directions when you couldn't see the design?

Was either partner feeling frustrated or annoyed? Why did this occur?

e. How do you think it feels to a student to experience this kind of frustration in school, on the playing field or with friends because of differences in the way he or she learns?

f. How do you think we can assist our classmates who are experiencing this kind of frustration in the classroom?

The Classroom as a Team

Purpose

To encourage classroom support for the child who evidences learning, social or behavioral problems.

Note

This theme may be used independent of the guide. You will note that the discussion questions are reflective of Theme VII. It serves to encourage the class to function as a support system for a child who engages in inappropriate behaviors, has difficulty relating to peers or is rejected by classmates. This team process has proven useful in building cooperation and understanding on the part of the class for the child whose behaviors may provoke conflict, confusion or concern. The procedures may be implemented by the classroom teacher, guidance counselor or other specialist who has been working with the student. Consultation among faculty members involved with the child may prove helpful in preparing for this presentation.

Objectives

The class will be able to:

1. Identify specific school situations that may be problematic for a particular student.
2. Generate thoughtful suggestions designed to support the child who experiences significant problems in relating to peers.

Preparatory Suggestions

It is suggested that the parents of the student who will be assisted in this program be contacted and informed of the process. Permission to proceed should be obtained. Prior to meeting with the class, the teacher should conference with the student to discuss the aspects of school that are most stressful to the child. Explain that you would like to speak to the class without the child present to discuss ways in which they can all work together as a team to help him to feel more comfortable in the classroom. Assure the child that he will be an important part of the team. Ask the student to generate ideas that would be beneficial in helping him to make and keep friends. Explain that after your class session you will share the class ideas with him. Tell him that there will be follow-up sessions to discuss the progress and develop new ideas. When progress is made and the student and class are relating well, he may be present for the class discussion if he wishes.

Presentation Suggestions

Introduction

Many of us have noticed and have been concerned about the difficulties that _____ has been having in the classroom. We are going to have an opportuntity to work together to help _____ feel more comfortable in school and learn new ways to make friends. We will be working together as a team to help this come about. Before we develop our team plans to help _____ , I have a few thoughts that I would like you to consider.

Discussion Questions

    a.   Look around the class. Is anyone here exactly the same as anyone else? Is there anyone who is just like you in this school? In this town? In the state? In the entire world?

    b.   Might there be any two people who are identical?

    c.   Are identical twins exactly alike in every way?

    d.   Would identical twins always want to play the same games, read the same books, eat the same food or play with the same friends?

    e.   Why are even identical twins different in some ways?

           Explain that everyone's brain, just like everyone's fingerprints, is somewhat different. Because our brains are unique to us, as are our experiences, we all learn and think in our own special ways. Each of us have areas that come easily to us and that we especially enjoy, and we each have areas that are challenging or difficult. (As the teacher and model, share those areas with the class that are pleasant for you. Discuss also those that are most difficult.)

    f.   What areas or activities do you especially enjoy or find to be easy?

    g.   What areas or activities do you find to be more difficult or challenging?

Note: These questions are a condensation of Theme VII.

Understanding the Child in Need

a. What areas do you think are especially difficult for _____ ?

b. What behaviors do we see that tell us that these areas are difficult? (Encourage the children not to pass value judgments but to be objective in their descriptions.) Make a list of these behaviors.

c. When are these behaviors most likely to occur?

d. Where do they most often occur?

e. Do you notice any patterns such as difficulties during particularly noisy or unstructured times? Are there usually problems for _____ during particular activities?

f. What have our responses been when these behaviors occur?

g. What activities does _____ especially enjoy? In what activities does _____ do well?

h. Explain to the class why the student may be exhibiting difficulties based on the child's learning style. Attentional problems, sensitivity to visual and auditory stimuli, and need of support in developing social skills may also affect behaviors.

Brainstorming Supportive Ideas

Let's make a list of suggestions that may help _____ feel more a part of this classroom.

a. How can we help _____ make and keep friends?

b. In what ways can _____ use his strengths to help us in the classroom?

c. How can we help _____ feel better about himself?

d. How can we help to make a positive difference in _____ life?

Follow-Up Activities

a. Meet with the student to review the insights and suggestions of the class. Ask him how he feels about the ideas.

b. Explain that you will all be working together as a team to improve the student's comfort level in the class and that the class is enthusiastic about his being a member of the team.

c. Meet with the class in a week to discuss the progress that has been made. Explain that there will be follow-up meetings to discuss further progress and suggestions.

d. Encourage the class members to request assistance of the team should any of them feel a need for support.

Appendices

Appendix A
Plain Talk About Learning Disabilities

Appendix B
Learning Style Preference

Appendix C
Vase and Profiles

Appendix D
White and Black Crosses

Appendix E
Visual Discrimination Challenge

Appendix F
Visual Memory

Appendix G
Blackboard Note

Appendix H
Visual-Motor Integration

Appendix I
Auditory-Visual-Motor Integration

"PLAIN" TALK about children with Learning Disabilities

NATIONAL INSTITUTE OF MENTAL HEALTH ● Division of Scientific and Public Information ● Plain Talk Series ● Hilda Fried, Editor

"Why does he read SAW for WAS?"

"Can't he see the difference between b and d?"

"How come she could read all of those words yesterday, and she can't get a single one today?"

"Will he never learn the days of the week?"

"If he can talk about life on Mars, why can't he add 2 × 2?"

"Can't he stop talking for 5 minutes?"

"She wasn't still for a moment all day, but when I want her down here for dinner, I can't get her to stop what she's doing!"

"Good Lord, what will he do next!!"

"Why won't he behave at school?"

"How could she put down the same answer to four different arithmetic problems?"

"Will she ever get it all together?"

"He's so good and he tries so hard, why can't he learn?"

"Every year he has another birthday, but nothing seems to change except his age!"

WHO IS THIS CHILD?

Usually . . .
- This is an intelligent child who fails at school.
- This is the child who at school age reads "on" for "no," writes 41 for 14, p for d or q for b, and can't remember the sequence of letters that make up a word.
- This is the child who loses her homework, misplaces her book, doesn't know what day it is, or what year, or what season.
- This is the child who calls breakfast "lunch" . . . who is confused by "yesterday," "today," and "tomorrow," the child whose timing is always off.

Frequently . . .
- This is the child who can't picture things in his mind, who can't visualize or remember what he sees.
- This is the quiet child who bothers nobody in the classroom but does not learn.
- This is the older child whose language comes out jumbled, who stops and starts in the middle of a sentence or an idea . . . who talks about hopsitals, aminals, and emenies.

Sometimes
- This is the child who can add and multiply but not subtract or divide . . . who can do math in his head but can't write it down.

U.S. DEPARTMENT OF HEALTH AND HUMAN SERVICES Public Health Service ● Alcohol, Drug Abuse, and Mental Health Administration
5600 Fishers Lane, Rockville, Maryland 20857

Appendix A

- This is the child who skips words, omits them, or adds them when he is reading aloud.

The Learning Disabled Child Is a Child with Disorder.

Usually, the child with an intact nervous system is a well-organized little human being by school age. He has sorted, classified, categorized information into the proper mail boxes in his mind. He has achieved the maturation necessary to learn efficiently. By age 6, most youngsters are ready for formal education. The child is ready for teaching. His equipment can handle it; he has the tools to do the job.

The learning disabled youngster is not ready on time. He is disorganized. He is consumed by DISORDER. He is *immature* rather than *abnormal*. A doctor would say that he suffers from neurological immaturity or minimal brain dysfunction. An educator would say that he has a learning disability. A parent would say: "Something is wrong."

The learning disabled child can't make sense of what he receives through his senses, even though his sight, hearing, and other sense organs are all intact. The messages he receives are jumbled, scattered all over the place. He is distracted which most people think is not paying attention, but, in fact, he is paying too much attention to too many things. At age 7 or 8 he is frequently very similar in his social behavior to the 2- and 3-year-old. He craves center stage, not out of any base ambitions but because of immaturity. He seems to need constant recognition of his existence long after the preschool years are over. Because of his many difficulties (with tying shoe laces, organization of speech, reading), he is dependent longer on the adults around him and must call for help over a longer period of time. The need for attention may equal the need for help, and many a learning disabled youngster has cleverly discovered that helplessness brings swift attention. Also, there are many children who would so much rather receive negative attention than no attention that they will purposely get in trouble or "act out" to evoke an adult response. Often they would rather be thought of as "bad" than "dumb." Some youngsters will provoke trouble with other children to make sure they are not ignored; they can then complain about being teased or picked on, but they have been the center of everyone's attention. This happens frequently with learning disabled youngsters.

The Learning Disabled Youngster Tends to Become Rigid and Inflexible

He is reminiscent of a very young child who cannot deal with alternatives at the immature level of his age. He becomes anxious when he is taken to the park by a new, unfamiliar route. He is upset on a Sunday morning when his parents have breakfast in their pajamas—breaking the known routine of dress first, breakfast afterward. He won't accept a broken cookie, because a cookie is round; if the broken piece is jagged, it can't be a cookie. He doesn't recognize a teacher outside of school. He may appear paralyzed when faced with two equal choices, unable to select either one.

The inflexible child who wants what he wants when he wants it, no matter what is going on around him—a storm, a riot, an accident, a crisis—is the same child who doesn't see the wholeness of things. He gets caught up in the details and misses the big picture.

Lost in Time and Space

The learning disabled child is most often lost in space—lost in up-down, left-right, above-below, top-bottom, in-out, into-out of, under-over, apart-together. He does not automatically know how to operate in space; he cannot visualize spaces. How can he know where the top shelf is if he is not sure that his feet are below his head?

He can't remember where to go, frequently gets lost, loses not only himself but his possessions, and doesn't see things that are right in front of his nose. Often when he's asked to stand in front of his desk, he stands behind it. Frequently he's asked to put the paper into the box, and he puts it under the box.

This is why clearly defined spaces, or small spaces, spell safety to the learning disabled child. This is why security depends on the same seat at the dining room table, the same place in the car, the same chair at school. A learning disabled child usually has a poor image of his own body. He does not connect the parts to the whole body. He does not know how far it extends or how much space it takes up. His development in this respect lags way behind what is usual for his chronological age. Frequently the learning disabled child is awkward and clumsy.

Clumsiness is:

MISJUDGING—*overdoing, underdoing, off balance*
POOR TIMING—*too fast, too slow*
NOT LOOKING
NOT LISTENING
NOT BEING ABLE TO COORDINATE
    SEVERAL THINGS AT ONCE

Free Spirit

There's a sheer joy—temporary though it may be—that many a learning disabled child brings to life. He seems to embrace life with an enthusiasm and jauntiness that most of us lose with maturity. The spontaneous expression of feeling, the unedited comment, the untrampled-upon gesture are all trademarks of the impulsive child. There's a freshness which he conveys, perhaps because he doesn't see the whole picture, that turns our attention to experiences we have come to take for granted. In the midst of checking the route map, watching the road signs, estimating when the next gas stop must be made, our attention is suddenly diverted to an unexpected delight when the learning disabled child remarks: "How fresh and good the grass smells!" With all the heartache he feels and brings into his home, he often touches the family with a freshness, a pure, natural quality.

Adapted from NO EASY ANSWERS—THE LEARNING DISABLED CHILD, an NIMH publication written by Sally L. Smith, Associate Professor, American University.
DHHS Publication No. (ADM) 80-825
Printed 1979 Reprinted 1980

Learning Style Preference

Name _____ Date_____

1. A. I like to get things done quickly.
   B. I like to take my time on a project and work carefully.

2. A. I enjoy expressing my thoughts in writing.
   B. I prefer to express myself in discussion or debate.

3. A. I seem to learn best when I work alone.
   B. I seem to learn best when I work with others in a small group.

4. A. I like to write a book report after reading a book.
   B. I prefer designing a diorama or poster to describe the book.

5. A. I like to see pictures of what I'm learning about.
   B. I would rather listen to stories about a subject than see pictures about it.
   C. I enjoy seeing pictures and listening to stories at the same time.

6. A. When I think, my thoughts usually come in words.
   B. When I think, my thoughts usually come in pictures.

7. A. I remember the messages that I hear.
   B. I like to write down the messages to help me remember.

8. A. I enjoy reading for pleasure.
   B. Given a choice, I would rather do a puzzle, build a model, or design a project instead of reading.

9. A. During free time I like to read, draw, or write.
   B. During free time I prefer to be physically active and play a sport or a game.

10. A. I like to watch, think, and plan before starting an activity.
    B. I like to become involved in the activity immediately.

Draw a picture or write a description of your favorite activity.

Do you think you learn best by:
   a. listening
   b. watching
   c. doing?

Appendix B

Appendix C

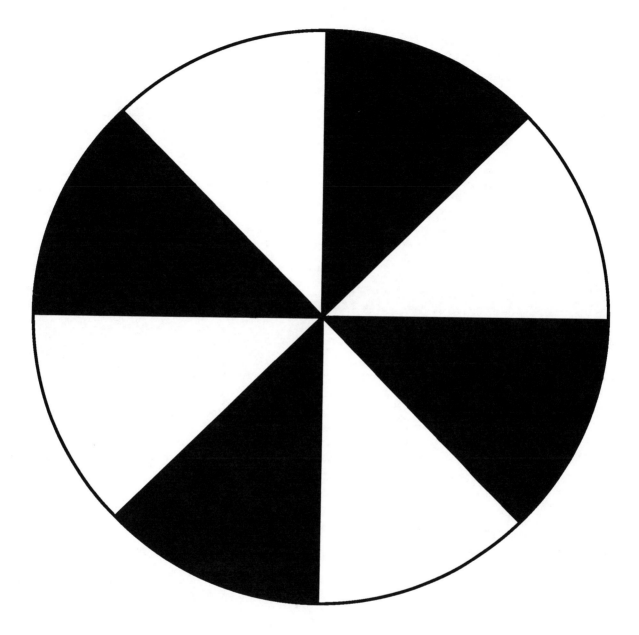

Appendix D

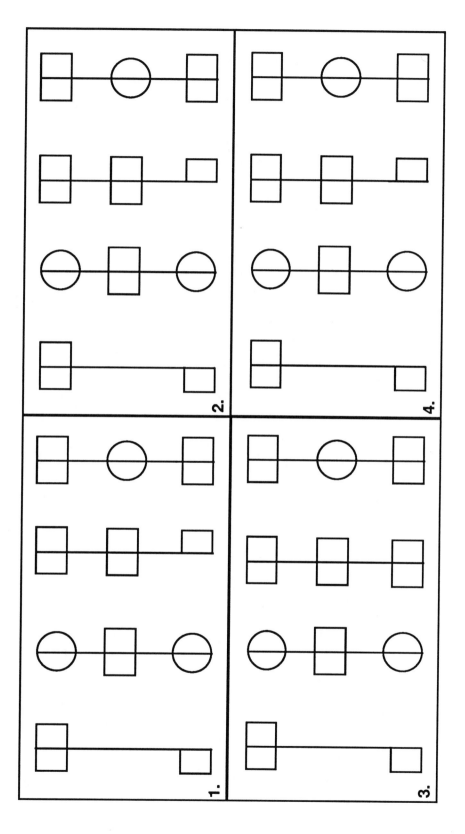

Appendix E

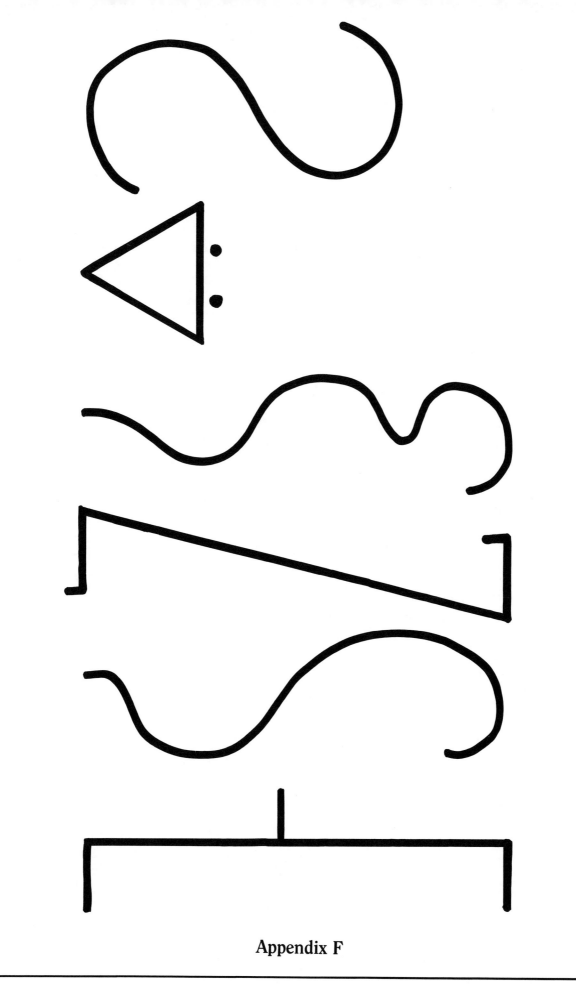

Appendix G

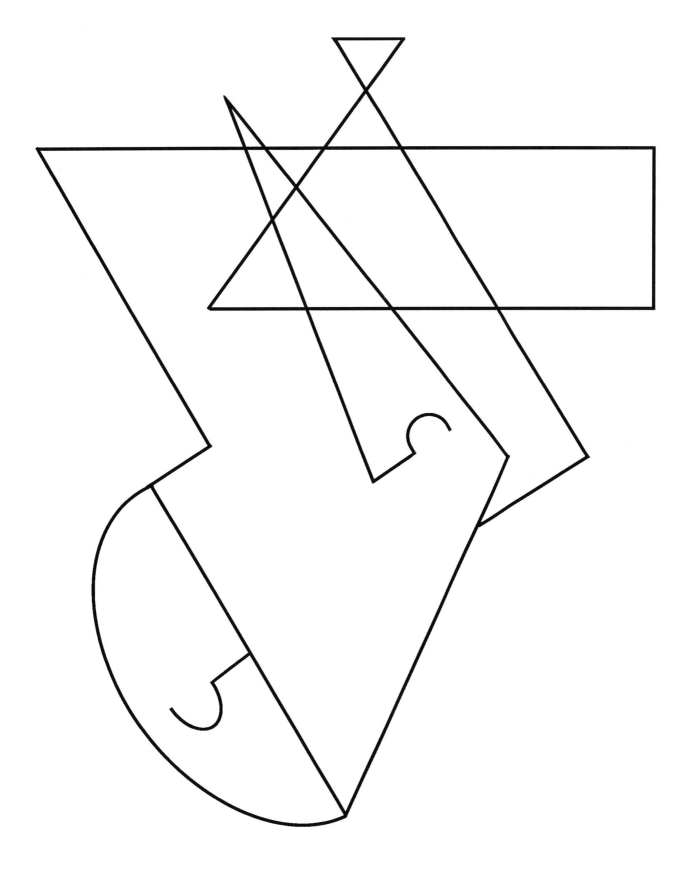

Appendix H

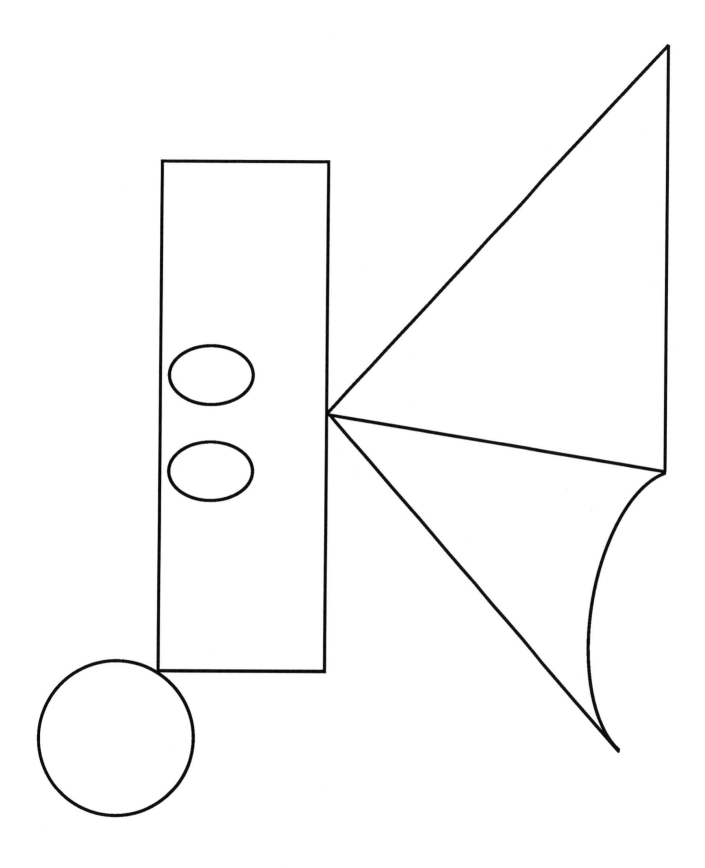

Appendix I-1

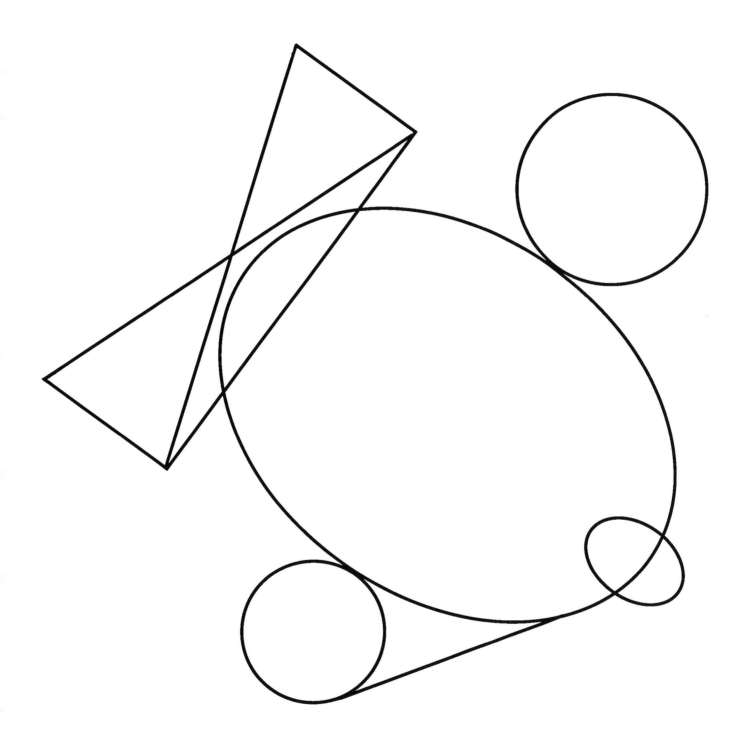

Appendix I-2

Work Samples

Special Pleasures
Theme VI: Activity A

Special Pleasures
Theme VI: Activity A

Who I Am Makes a Difference
Theme VI: Follow-Up Activity

Who I Am Makes a Difference
Theme VI: Follow-Up Activity

Student Evaluation of I Make a Difference!

Letter from the Future

Letter from the Future

Soccer

bike rideing

Swimming

skiing

Danceing

bowling

ice skating

math
$\begin{array}{r} 9 \\ \times 8 \\ \hline 73 \end{array}$ $\begin{array}{r} 9 \\ \times 9 \\ \hline 81 \end{array}$

water skiing

gym

reading books

cheerleading

Singing

Special Pleasures
Theme VI: Activity A (page 46, 47)

Who I AM Makes

I help my mother a lot

I am participating in "C.A.R.E." which may help people a lot when published.

I play in the band.

I discuss books with older people (which they really enjoy).

I made an Earth Day Poster

I help people when they need it!

I take care of my dog.

I help teach people things but they don't know who everybody else teaches.

IM ME

If I read a book that I like I will recommend it to someone.

I make friends with everybody

I bring joy to my family.

I have gotten many pledges for my Walk for Hunger

I lit a candle for a living thing.

Marc

A Difference!

Sarah Hess   C.A.R.E.   June 13, 1990

1. I found that C.A.R.E. was personally helpful in sports groups, Girl Scouts and summer camp groups because I can get along with people nicely.

2. I think C.A.R.E. did help the class because we learned to respect and be friends with eachother.

3. The parts I enjoyed most about C.A.R.E. were the skits and plays and the two guest speakers: Chris Greenwood and Carroll Spinney.

4. I think the idea I had was already discussed. It was to put in a play about teasing so students could feel what it's like to be teased.

Thank you, Mrs. Tamaren,
for coming!
Your C.A.R.E. student

Sarah

Student Evaluation of I Make a Difference!

6/7/2005

Dear Mrs. Tamaren,
I got out of Yale a week ago, and I've just been drafted for the Toronto Blue Jays.
If it was not for you I would probly not be in this ball club. It was the C. A. R. E. lessons that you tought that told me to 'stick with my dream.
I am playing for the Toronto Blue Jays, because it been a life goal and also become succuseful.

Your friend
Bryan Manter,

P.S. During spring break I umpire Little leage games.

July 16, 200X

Dear Mrs. Tamaren,

Hi! (This is from Kara House) How are you? I have ended another year of college and have been placing an ad in the paper advertising my practicing of being a commercial artist and have gotten two jobs for designing a chinese resteraunt menu, and for a hair salon. I write a small comic strip for our local paper, entitled "The Family". Why did I pick these jobs? Because I love designing menus and ads, and being creative and funny. I also love making people laugh, or be cheery, after a hard day when they settle down with the paper and, hopefully, read my comic. I am even majoring in commercial Arts. C.A.R.E. has helped me for a long time. I once ran a small playgroup where we taught kids all about teasing, autism, prejudice and the resource room. I hope I affected the lives of those kids who are about 10 now like you have influenced our class.

I am also studying to be a Nursery School teacher. I want to tell small kids what they need to know and then some. I want to influence hundreds of kids and have them remember me like I remember my teachers. That is, how much they taught me.

Your C.A.R.E. student,
Kara S. House
(Commercial Artist)

References and Resources

Bandura, A. and Walters, R.H. 1963. *Social learning and personality development.* New York: Holt, Rinehart, and Winston.

Borba, M and C. 1982. *Self-esteem: A classroom affair (100 ways to help children like themselves).* Minneapolis, MN: Winston Press.

Borba, M. and C. 1982. *Self-esteem: A classroom affair (More ways to help children like themselves).* Volume 2, Minneapolis, MN: Winston Press.

Bronfenbrenner, U. 1979. *The ecology of human development.* Cambridge, MA: Harvard University Press.

Brooks, R. 1991. *The self-esteem teacher.* Circle Pines, MN: American Guidance Service.

Bryan, T.H. 1986. Self-concept and attributions of the learning disabled. *Learning Disabilities Focus,* Vol. 1, Number 2, Spring.

Bryan, T.H., Cosden, M., and Pearl, R. 1982. The effects of cooperative models on learning disabled and nonlearning disabled students. *Learning Disabled Quarterly,* Vol. 5, pp. 415-421.

Bulifant, J. *Gifts of greatness:* Videotape. Landmark West School, 11450 Port Road, Culver City, CA 90230.

Buscaglia, L. 1971. Love as a behavior modifier. Dallas, Texas: Presentation to the Texas Association for Children and Adults with Learning Disabilities.

Campbell, P. and Siperstein, G. 1989. *Improving social competence: Techniques for teachers.* Boston: University of MA.

Canfield, J. 1986. *Self-esteem in the classroom.* Pacific Palisades, CA: Self-Esteem Seminars.

Davidson, H.H. and Lang, G. 1960. Children's perceptions of their teachers' feelings toward them related to self-perception, school achievement, and behavior. *Journal of Experimental Education,* 29, pp. 107-118.

Gallagher, B. 1967. The effect of teacher attitudes on children's response to defective articulation. *Journal of Educational Research,* 60, pp. 456-458.

Gallet, J. The judge who could not tell his right from his left and other tales of learning disabilities. Lecture at the Law School of the State University of New York at Buffalo.

Garrett, M.K. and Grump, W.E. 1980. Peer acceptance, teacher preference, and self-approval of social status among learning disabled students. *Learning Disabilities Quarterly,* 3, pp. 42-48.

Good, T.L. and Brophy, J. 1974. Changing teacher and student behavior: An empirical investigation. *Journal of Educational Psychology,* 66, pp. 340-405.

Issacs, S. and Ritchey, W. 1989. *I think I can, I know I can.* New York: St. Martin's Press.

Kaplowitz, M.L. 1981 *Self-concept of mainstreamed learning disabled children in resource room and regular classrooms.* Boston: Boston University.

LeShan, E. 1976. *In search of myself and other children.* NY: St. Martin's Press.

Levine, M. 1990. *Keeping a head in school.* Cambridge, MA: Educators Publishing Service.

McGinnis, A.L. 1990 *The power of optimism.* San Francisco: Harper and Row Publishers.

Montagu, A. 1971. *Touching: The human significance of skin.* NY: Columbia University Press.

Osman, B.B. 1982. *No one to play with: The social side of learning disabilities.* Novato, CA: Academic Therapy Publications.

Purkey, W. 1970. *Self-concept and school achievement.* Englewood Cliffs, NJ: Prentice-Hall, Inc.

Richardson, B.O. and Dalton, J.L. 1973. Teacher rating and self-concept reports of retarded pupils. *Exceptional Children,* 40, pp. 178-183.

Rosser, G.J. 1974. A comparative analysis of real-ideal self-concept of nondisabled and language and/or learning disabled children. *Dissertation Abstracts International,* 36, pp. 679-680.

Seaman, J. 1973. Self-concept, social acceptance and teacher attitudes related to the treatment of children labeled as perceptually handicapped. University of Pittsburg.

Segal, J. 1988. Teachers have enormous power in affecting a child's self-esteem. *The Brown University Child Behavior and Development Letter,* 4, pp. 1-3.

Simpson, E. 1979. *Reversals: A personal account of victory over dyslexia.* Boston: Houghton Mifflin Co.

Siperstein, G. and Goding, J. 1983. Social integration of learning disabled children in regular classrooms. *Advances in Learning and Behavioral Disabilities.* Ed. K.G. Gadow and I. Bailer. Greenwich, CT: GAI Press. pp. 227-263.

Siperstein, G. and Gottlieb, J. 1977. Physical stigma and academic performance as factors affecting children's first impressions of handicapped peers. *American Journal of Mental Deficiency,* 81, pp. 455-462.

Toffler, A. 1971. *Future Shock.* NY: Bantam Books.

Vail, P. 1987. *Smart kids with school problems: Things to know and ways to help.* NY: E.P. Dutton.

Weiner, B. 1974. *Achievement motivation and attribution theory.* Morristown, NJ: General Learning Press.

Weinstein, R.S. 1982. Expectations in the classroom: The student perspective. NY: Invited address, annual conference of the American Educational Research Association.